Creative
Paint & Embroidery
ON FABRIC

by JULIE NEILSON-KELLY

A J.B. Fairfax Press Publication

CONTENTS

CONTENTS

This book is dedicated to the memory of my friend and student, Mary Swain.
We shared birthdays and our love for creativity and beautiful things.
'To know her was to love her.'

EDITORIAL
Managing Editor: Judy Poulos
Editorial Assistant: Ella Martin
Photography: Richard Weinstein,
Clayton Glenn
Styling: Kathy Tripp, Bronte Camillari
DESIGN AND PRODUCTION
Production Director: Anna Maguire
Production Coordinator: Meredith Johnson
Design Manager: Drew Buckmaster
Production Editor: Lulu Dougherty
Editorial and Production
Assistant: Heather Straton
Published by J.B. Fairfax Press Pty Limited
80-82 McLachlan Ave
Rushcutters Bay NSW 2011, Australia
A.C.N. 003 738 430

Formatted by J.B. Fairfax Press Pty Limited
Printed by Toppan Printing Company,
Singapore

JBFP 505
CREATIVE PAINT & EMBROIDERY ON FABRIC
ISBN 1 86343 331 7

DISTRIBUTION AND SALES
Australia: J.B. Fairfax Press
Ph: (02) 9361 6366 Fax: (02) 9360 6262
Web: http://www.jbfp.com.au
USA: Quilters' Resource Inc
2211 North Elston Ave
Chicago, Ill 60614
Ph: (773) 278 5695 Fax: (773) 278 1348

ABOUT THE AUTHOR

Paint and Embroidery on Fabric is Julie's third book in the Creative Series. Her first book *Inspirations in Paint* was written to include technical advice for the painter, along with details for observation and construction in painting floral designs for decorative art. It is an ideal companion book to *Paint and Embroidery on Fabric*. *Creative Tassels* was co-authored by Julie with Madeleine Willingham and featured wonderful illustrations by Julie's husband, Malcolm Kelly, who has again provided the diagrams for the stitch glossary for this book.

Julie travels extensively conducting workshops in many varied arts and crafts. She continues to design giftwrap and découpage papers with varying subjects including florals, country themes and collectables, such as teddy bears, dolls and antique toys. Recently, she moved into the production of prints and cards of her beautifully hand-painted designs.

Over the past couple of years, she has made guest appearances on some of Australia's best known television programs, being featured on special segments and conducting 'How to' presentations for craft subjects, as well as continuing to write articles and design projects for magazines. Julie also offers a worldwide mail order service for her kits.

INTRODUCTION

I have written this book with a view to offering inspiration to the painter and embroiderer alike. I would like to encourage them to look further afield and experiment with new and different ideas, to bring an artistic impression to the exciting combination of paints, fabrics, threads and textures.

I have included information on creating stencils and theorem painting on fabric. As a teacher, I have found that many students, lacking confidence with freehand painting, find these alternative methods most creative and rewarding.

Please take into account that all the designs in the book can be enlarged or reduced to a size suitable for the project of your choice. The finished project featured in the book is just a suggestion for its use. Each piece is suitable for many different finishes.

Each project is accompanied by a full-size design illustration, which gives you the line drawing for the painting, a shaded area for depth points, and a placement and stitch guide for the embroidery.

The stitch glossary at the back of the book describes and illustrates the stitches you can use to embellish your work. You will see how exciting the combination of painting and embroidery can be.

In this book, I have put together a wide variety of projects. All the products to complete these projects are widely available. In addition, all the projects are available in either kit form by mail order, or in a workshop situation from my studio. For anyone requiring further information, please write to me at Artistic Renditions, PO Box 242, Glenside, South Australia 5065 or fax on (08) 8332 8317.

I wish you many hours of enjoyment and success with your projects and I am sure you will find great satisfaction in your achievements.

Julie

GETTING STARTED

Painting on fabric is quite different from painting on a non-porous surface. Fabric is unforgiving in that mistakes cannot be wiped away, so practice is required to achieve the desired result.

Painting with solid colour requires a slight build-up of paint to make a surface in which to blend. This technique is used for most painting projects in the book. Some great effects can also be achieved with very watery colour washes.

These effects can be used for backgrounds, and provide interesting bases for embroidery.

EXERCISES

Stretch some calico and hold it firmly in place on the work surface. Prepare your palette with a depth colour such as Paynes Gray. Mix the paint with the textile medium as directed on the bottle, before applying it to the fabric.

Practise loading a ¹/₂" flat chisel brush with paint in the following way:
1 Dampen the brush, keeping the brush flat.
2 Load anticlockwise through the paint for depth of colour on one side, fading across to nothing on the other side.
3 Apply paint to the fabric and practise the strokes shown in Details1, 2, 5 and 6. The right consistency and ratio of paint to water comes with practice.
4 At this stage, you could also try the water wash technique shown in Detail 3: Load the brush with a watery, transparent consistency of paint and apply it liberally to the surface, spreading the watery colour as you go.

5 For a padded wash (Detail 4), apply a watery wash but pad out the areas with a rag or paper towel for a textured appearance.
6 Using a liner brush, practise linear shading as shown in Detail 7, using the tip of the brush for lining up and fine detail. This brush can also be used to create a stipple effect in certain areas by using the point in a staccato fashion (Detail 8). Special stipple brushes are also available.

All of these paint application methods can be used in a scene such as Jessie's House on page 10. Many of them are used for the painted backgrounds, such as for Autumn Leaves on page 15. Shaded loads, such as shown in Detail 1, are best for painting skin tone and contours, as well as for the floral designs.

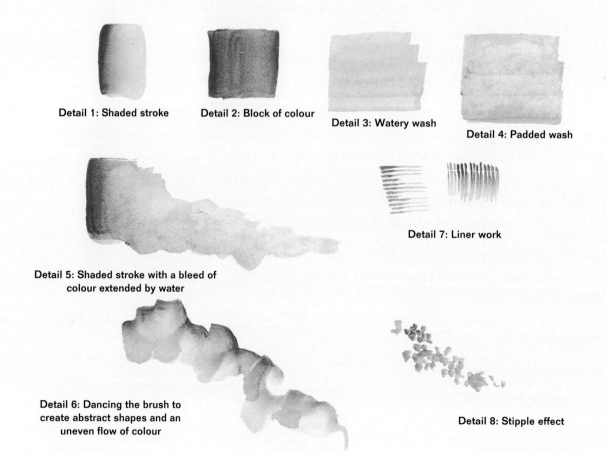

Detail 1: Shaded stroke

Detail 2: Block of colour

Detail 3: Watery wash

Detail 4: Padded wash

Detail 7: Liner work

Detail 5: Shaded stroke with a bleed of colour extended by water

Detail 6: Dancing the brush to create abstract shapes and an uneven flow of colour

Detail 8: Stipple effect

MATERIALS

FABRIC

There are many types of fabric suitable for painting on – from calico to silk– and so many wonderful textures to experiment with. Take into account how you visualise the finished piece and explore the possibilities, before making the final decision.

Calico is a good choice when first attempting to paint on fabric as it is inexpensive, extremely versatile and has a unique beauty. There are many different grades of calico. It is a very underestimated fabric.

It is beneficial to wash the calico before you begin, to remove the size and allow shrinkage to take place. This is especially relevant if the item might need to be laundered later. After it is washed and dried, calico will need to be ironed and can be attached to a frame for stretching. You can make a simple frame or you could stretch the fabric over an old picture frame, securing it with small tacks or pins, or even stapling it in place.

An alternative to stretching a fabric taut in a frame is to tape it firmly to a board with masking tape, or back the fabric with a contact adhesive. Ultimately, which method will work best will depend on what you are painting, as well as the availability of materials and personal choice.

PAINTS

As with most mediums, there is a variety of products to choose from. I use acrylic paints mixed with a fabric medium. I find that this works well for me. I like to use certain colours in my fabric painting that carry through from the painting of other surfaces. Using the same paints assures me of this continuity, which is important when coordinating items for interior design work and so on. It is also far more satisfactory and economical to have a range of paints which will serve many purposes, instead of a different range for each job. Acrylic paints are water-based products which are easy to work with, easy to mix and easy to clean up.

Throughout this book I have listed the colours for acrylic paints in the Jo Sonja range and the oil paints in the Winsor and Newton range. If you are unable to obtain these brands, please use my colours as a guide; conversion charts and books are available. The same colour or one that is very similar in another brand will serve the same purpose and this is all part of improvising and experimenting – two things I am very fond of doing.

TEXTILE MEDIUM

I prefer to use Jo Sonja's Textile Medium to mix with my paints, regardless of the colour or brand of the paint. The textile medium gives an ease of painting and allows the bond of fabric and paint to be heat-set, rendering the work suitable for laundering.

It is important that the paint application properly penetrates the fibres of the fabric.

Paint mixed with the textile medium will not store well, so mix the colours only as you need them.

For best results, always follow the manufacturer's instructions.

BRUSHES

I use chisel edge or flat brushes for all my painting, so a variety of sizes, ranging from $1/8$" to 1" is always handy to have.

Most work in this book has been painted using a $1/2$" flat brush, with the occasional round brush and liner where necessary. I use a synthetic brush for fabric painting as I find the application with this type of brush most successful.

LIGHT BOX

A light box is very handy if you are working with a design, where you plan your design on paper before transferring it to fabric.

Begin by sketching out your ideas and placement, marking in areas to which you may later wish to add another dimension, such as embroidery or appliqué. If you plan your work in this way, you can make good use of the light box in helping you through the different stages.

Place your sketch on the light box with the fabric taped over the top. You can then transfer the design with an HB pencil, without troublesome sketch lines.

If you don't have access to a light box, you can tape the design and the fabric to a window with the light coming through it and trace the design. This will serve the same purpose.

OTHER ITEMS

Iron An iron is needed to heat-set your work. Remember to use a cloth or tissue paper to protect your work and preferably iron it on the back.

Ceramic tile or china plate I always mix on a hard palette, such as a ceramic tile or china plate, and prefer to use a flexible palette knife.

White paper A sheet of clean, white paper is needed for placing under the fabric while it is being painted.

CUSHIONS

Rather than giving instructions for making the specific cushions, here are some general instructions for a 38 cm (15 in) square cushion with a ruffle, which you can adapt to suit.

MATERIALS

80 cm (32 in) of fabric
Matching sewing thread
Jeans needle for the machine
Three buttons
Crochet cotton
Ruler
2B pencil or tailor's chalk
Paper for the pattern
Usual sewing supplies
40 cm (16 in) cushion insert

PREPARATION

STEP ONE

Draw and cut out a 38 cm (15 in) square from paper. Cut one corner in a gentle curve. Fold this over each of the other three corners in turn and trim them to match. This is the pattern for the front. Curving the corners makes attaching piping or a ruffle much easier.

STEP TWO

For the pattern for the back, fold another sheet of paper in half. Draw a line 4 cm (1½ in) from the fold. Fold the front pattern in half and place this fold parallel to the fold on the plain sheet of paper, on the drawn line. Trace the cushion pattern onto the plain sheet of paper. Opening this new template out will give you a rectangle approximately 38 cm x 48 cm (15 in x 19 in) with gently rounded corners.
Note: This method will work for cushions of all shapes.

CUTTING

STEP ONE

Place the cushion patterns across the width of the fabric, along one cut edge. Cut one front and two backs.

STEP TWO

Using the tailor's chalk, mark two 10 cm (4 in) strips across the width of the fabric for the ruffle, skimming the cushion front and backs. The total length of the strips should be twice the circumference of the cushion.

CONSTRUCTION

STEP ONE

If the fabric is soft with little body, it is a good idea to back it with a stabiliser. Iron-on interfacing works well and also helps to prevent fraying.

STEP TWO

Press the two back pieces over double, with the wrong sides facing.

STEP THREE

Join the sections of the ruffle together to form a loop. Press the seams open, then press the strip over double. Using a wide zigzag and the jeans needle, stitch around the edges over the crochet cotton, taking care not to catch the cotton. Later, you will be able to pull up the crochet cotton to gather the ruffle. No more broken gathering threads!

STEP FOUR

Divide the ruffle into quarters and mark these points with a pin. Pull up the crochet cotton to fit the cushion. Placing each of the pins at a corner of the front, pin the ruffle to the front with the raw edges matching and the ruffle lying towards the middle. Allow extra gathers at the corners. Using a slightly longer than usual straight stitch (easier to unpick), stitch the ruffle in place.

STEP FIVE

Mark three points along the fold on one back section and make three buttonholes. Sew three button to match on the other back piece. Overlap the two back sections, with the buttonholes on top, so they form a 38 cm (15 in) square. Baste the overlap in place.

STEP SIX

Place the front and back together with the right sides facing and the ruffle in between. Stitch around the edge. Overlock the raw edges together. Turn the cover through and check the corners and gathers. Slip the insert inside.
Note: The insert should always be a few centimetres (an inch) larger than the finished cover.

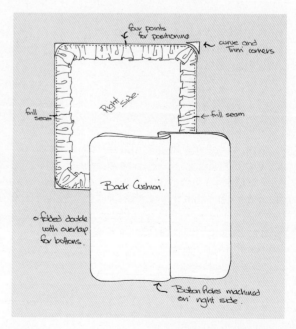

PAINTED BACKGROUNDS

'Autumn leaves' and 'Poppies' feature the translation of glorious photographic images onto a canvas with painted backgrounds. 'Thread painting' is used for the actual subject.

Both pieces have been beautifully embroidered by Mary Jaquier, who has translated the photography of Susan Taylor into a finished piece of art. Susan's photography captures the essential beauty of the landscape and has been used by Mary as the inspiration for many of her pieces.

The inspiration for 'Jessie's House' on page 10 came from Jessie Fowler's beautiful English house and garden. Sue Turrell has represented her grandmother's gorgeous garden with many creative stitches. We painted the background of the house and the greenery onto the fabric, using various applications, as shown in the exercises for practice on page 6.

USING A PHOTOGRAPH

A very clear photograph is ideal for translating into art work such as this.

To translate your own photographs, enlarge the image on a photocopier to the size required then, using a light box, trace around the contours of the main subject and other important areas onto the fabric.

You will be working in the negative space of the design (this is the area which is not your subject) when you start to paint. Paint in the background only, paying special attention to the mix of colours and textures. These effects can be created by referring to the application strokes on page 6. You can bleed colours into each other, you can pad colours out while they are wet and you can bring in strong, opaque colour where depth is needed. You can line up areas to create back interest and detail or leave very washy effects for softness. The shapes that you have chosen as your main focal points will be left unpainted for the embroidery or thread painting.

THREAD PAINTING

Thread painting is the method of blending long and short straight stitches together at random to create a blend of colours that are as lifelike as possible. When creating this blend of colours, it is important to strictly follow the photograph for detail of changing colours, highlights and depth areas. Attention to detail and shading is especially important for thread painting.

While the same stitch is basically used for the whole design, there are many instances when another texture could look interesting. For example, if you were thread painting a flower with stamens, French knots or even small beads would create extra height and interest in this area.

Work methodically across and through your work, taking care that you give a nice, even effect to the embroidery. Make sure you create a solid edge. To do this, you could first run a back stitch around the edge of the subject. Work each row well into the previous row. The process is quite time-consuming, but once you get 'on a roll' with it, the area will fill up quite quickly, and it certainly gives a rewarding and beautiful result.

The painted background for poppies.

A clear, coloured photograph is a useful aid.

JESSIE'S HOUSE

Inspired by old English cottages and her grandmother's house, Sue Turrell has created this beautiful painted house in an embroidered garden with a painted background.

Parts of the garden have been extended onto the picture mount, which gives added emphasis to the embroidery. It is an optional finish to your piece, once it is framed. If you would like to paint the extension, have your embroidery stretched and mounted, then, using paints in the same colours as the embroidery threads, continue the background colours in green washes across the mount. Create stipple effects to represent the flowers.

The applications used to paint the background are all given on page 6.

MATERIALS

For the painting
20 cm x 21 cm (8 in x 8¹/₄ in) of calico (the image area is 16 cm x 17 cm (6¹/₄ in x 6³/₄ in))
Light box (optional)
Sharp HB pencil
¹/₂" flat brush
Round brush or liner brush, size 0
Ruler
Jo Sonja's Textile Medium
Jo Sonja's Artists Acrylic Gouache: Raw Sienna, Burnt Sienna, Red Earth, Burnt Umber, Warm White, Paynes Gray, Pine Green
Jar of water
Palette
Clean white paper
Workboard
Masking tape
Rag
For the embroidery
Chenille needles, various sizes
Embroidery scissors
DMC Stranded Cotton: White; Black; Greens 368, 502, 503, 504, 520, 523, 640, 642, 782, 906, 987, 988, 3012, 3051, 3346, 3362; Blues 333, 341, 793; Yellows 677, 742, 745, 834, 973, 3041; Purples 819, 3014, 3042, 3753, 3942; Pinks 223, 224, 225, 778, 957, Burgundy 315; Red 3350
Anchor Marlitt Thread: Yellow 064, Green 1058
Appleton's Crewel Wool, Yellow 473

PREPARATION

See the painting design on the Pull Out Pattern Sheet.

STEP ONE

Using the pencil, lightly transfer the design to the fabric. A light box can make this easier. Refer to page 7 for the use of the light box or an alternative. Place the fabric over the clean white paper and tape it down on the workboard. Use the ruler to mark a straight border around the edge of the design. Keep the tracing soft, as hard pencil lines will not cover satisfactorily.

Use the ruler to mark a straight border around the edge of the design.

STEP TWO

Prepare the palette, mixing the textile medium with the paints following the manufacturer's instructions.

PAINTING

STEP ONE

Start painting the house, using the ¹/₂" brush, with Raw Sienna as the base and Burnt Sienna to create depth areas. Create the texture of the bricks with short, flat, staggered strokes in Red Earth. The roof is textured with similar strokes, using the Burnt Sienna.

STEP TWO

Paint the woodwork and window frames using the liner brush and Burnt Umber. Some of the window panes can have a touch of white added to them to give variety in the glass colour.

STEP THREE

Apply a watery, pale wash of Paynes Gray across the sky area and pad it out with the rag to give the effect of a cloudy sky.

STEP FOUR

Paint the trees behind the house in Pine Green, using the brush in a dancing motion to create the look of foliage.

STEP FIVE

Paint the front path, blending Raw Sienna and Burnt Sienna, and adding a touch of Pine Green for the shadows close to the path edge.

Paint the front lawn with Pine Green as a base for the embroidered garden. Stipple the climbing vines up the walls of the house in Pine Green. This will also act as a base for the embroidery. Paint in the background detail with the fine brush. Try to keep a straight firm line around the edge of the design. This will give you more options when framing your piece.

STEP SIX

Remove the paper from the back of the fabric so that it doesn't stick when the paint dries. Allow the painting to dry completely, then heat-set it by ironing on the back of the fabric. As this piece

is to be framed and never laundered, it is not imperative that you heat-set it; however, as a rule it is wise to do it and it will also flatten out your work for the embroidery process.

EMBROIDERY

See the embroidery design and key on page 14.

Note: I have used two strands of DMC Stranded Cotton, unless otherwise specified. The flowers correspond to the key. Each flower is completed, including the centres and stems.

BLUEBELLS

Work the petals in French knots, using 793 and the stems in straight stitch using 368.

CLIMBING ROSES

Work the petals in French knots using White and the stems in stem stitch using 640 and 642. The leaves are fly stitch in a single strand of Marlitt 1058.

DAFFODILS

Work the petals in lazy daisy stitch using 973 with pistil stitch centres in a single strand of 742. The stems are straight stitch in 520.

DAISIES

Work the dark yellow daisy petals in lazy daisy stitch, using 834, with French knot centres in six strands of Marlitt 064. The stems are straight stitch using 782.

Work the light yellow daisy petals in lazy daisy stitch, using 745, with French knot centres in a single strand of Appleton's 473. The stems are straight stitch using 3012.

Work the pink and light pink daisy petals in lazy daisy stitch, using a single strand of 778 and 819, with French knot centres in 3041 and 742. The stems are straight stitch using 3346.

Work the white daisy petals in lazy daisy stitch, using 2, with French knot centres in 677. The stems are straight stitch using 3362.

Simple stitches grouped close together create the impression of a garden.

Extend the embroidered garden onto the mount by painting flowers to look like stitches.

FOXGLOVES

Work the petals in straight stitch, using 957 and 819, using the lighter colour at the top and the darker colour towards the bottom. The stems are straight stitch using 987.

HOLLYHOCKS

Work the flowers in blanket stitch, using a single strand each of 223, 224 and 225, using the lightest colour at the top and shading towards the darkest colour at the bottom. The centres are French knots, using 315 and the leaves are lazy daisy stitch using 906.

BEARDED IRISES

Work the petals in lazy daisy stitch with straight stitch sides in a single strand of 793 and 333, alternating the colours. The stems are straight stitch using 3012 and 523, alternating the colours.

LAVENDER

Work the petals in bullion stitch, using a single strand of 3014 and 3042, alternating the colours. The leaves are fly stitch, using 504.

LOBELIA

Work the petals in French knots using a single strand each of 341 and 333, alternating the colours.

RED EYES

Work the petals in French knots using a single strand of 3350. The centres are French knots using a single strand of Black and the stems are straight stitch using 988 and 906.

SNOWDROPS

Work the petals in lazy daisy stitch using 2. The stems are straight stitch using 3362 and 3012.

SUNFLOWERS

Work the petals in lazy daisy stitch in Appletons 473. The centres are French knots using six strands of Black. The stems are straight stitch and the leaves are lazy daisy stitch using six strands of 3051.

VIOLAS

Work the petals in French knots using 3041 and 3753, alternating the colours. The stems are straight stitch using 520.

WISTERIA

Work the petals in French knots using 3041, 3942 and 819. The stems are straight stitch and the leaves are lazy daisy stitch in a single strand of 502, 503 and 504.

MAKING UP

When the embroidery is completed, have the picture professionally framed.

Remember, if you wish to continue the painted area over the mount, you will need to ask your picture framer to stretch and mount your piece so that you can complete the painting, before the picture is given its final frame.

Lazy daisy stitches, buttonhole stitches and French knots make sunflowers and hollyhocks.

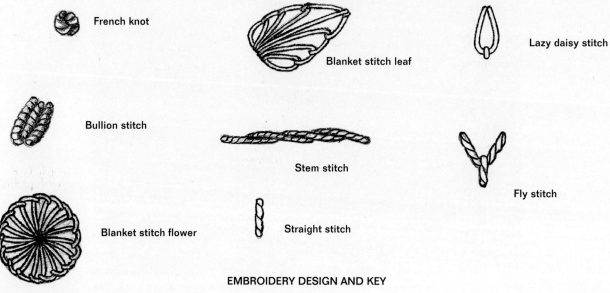

French knot

Blanket stitch leaf

Lazy daisy stitch

Bullion stitch

Stem stitch

Fly stitch

Blanket stitch flower

Straight stitch

EMBROIDERY DESIGN AND KEY

AUTUMN LEAVES

This is a glorious reflection of the changing seasons with its subtle blending of colours. The background fabric has been painted with acrylic colours to create depth and dimension.

Note: Working from a good colour photograph can be very helpful in creating a piece such as this one.

MATERIALS

For the painting
27 cm x 32 cm (10^1/$_2$ in x 12^1/$_2$ in) of calico
Sharp HB pencil
^{1}/$_2$" flat brush
Round brush or liner brush, size 0
Ruler
Jo Sonja's Textile Medium
Jo Sonja's Artists Acrylic Gouache: Pine Green, Teal Green, Burgundy
Jar of water
Palette
Clean white paper
Workboard
Masking tape
Light box (optional)

For the embroidery
Chenille needles
Embroidery scissors
Original photograph (optional)
Anchor Stranded Cotton: Pinks/Reds 10, 11, Greens 265, 259, 0889, 0375
DMC Stranded Cotton: Greens 471, 472, 833, 988, 989; Pinks/Reds 3830, 3777, 8838, Black

PREPARATION

See the painting design on the Pull Out Pattern Sheet.

STEP ONE

Using the pencil, lightly transfer the design to the fabric. A light box can make this easier. Refer to page 7 for the use of the light box or an alternative. Place the fabric over the clean white paper and tape it down on the workboard. Use the ruler to mark a straight border around the edge of the design.

STEP TWO

Prepare the palette, mixing the textile medium with the paints, following the manufacturer's instructions.

PAINTING

STEP ONE

Paint the background using the flat brush, creating texture and blending the colours. Remember, you are not painting the areas to be embroidered. Paint the detail, using the fine brush.

This beautiful photograph was the inspiration for the painted and embroidered piece.

Try to keep a straight, firm line around the edge of the design. This will give you options when framing your piece.

STEP TWO

Remove the paper from the back of the fabric so that it doesn't stick when the paint dries. Allow the painting to dry completely, then heat-set it by ironing on the back of the fabric. As this piece is to be framed and never laundered, it is not imperative that you heat-set it; however, as a rule it is wise to do it and it will also flatten out your work for the embroidery process.

EMBROIDERY

STEP ONE

Note: The entire thread painting is stitched using two strands of cotton.

Work the veins and the stems in a fine satin stitch, with the colours blending and changing as the photograph suggests. Use DMC 833, 8838 and Anchor 259, 0889 and 0375.

STEP TWO

The remainder of the design is the shaded leaf area. Shade the different colours as indicated in the photograph, using DMC 471, 472, 988, 989, 3830, 3777; Anchor 10, 11, 265 and working long and short straight stitches together to blend the colours. Attention to detail is important.

MAKING UP

Have your piece professionally framed for a really beautiful finish.

The painted background prior to embroidery.

Detail of the stitches and blending of colours.

POPPIES

The vibrant golds, yellows and oranges of the poppy have been brought to life with the sheen of Marlitt thread, stitched and blended to create shadows and form. The painted background adds interest and depth.

Note: This picture uses the same method as for 'Autumn Leaves' on page 15. As with that project, working from an original photograph can be helpful.

MATERIALS

For the painting

35 cm x 45 cm (14 in x 18 in) of calico
Sharp HB pencil
$1/2$" flat brush
Round brush or liner brush, size 0
Ruler
Jo Sonja's Textile Medium
Jo Sonja's Artists Acrylic Gouache:
    Pine Green, Teal Green, Paynes
    Gray, Diox Purple, Burgundy, Raw
    Sienna, Warm White
Jar of water
Palette
Clean white paper
Workboard
Masking tape
Light box (optional)

For the embroidery

Chenille needle
Embroidery scissors
Original photograph (optional)
DMC Stranded Cotton: Yellows R444,
    R307, R972; Greens 319, 471, 989,
    987, 367, 988, 870, 3345
Anchor Marlitt Rayon Thread:
    Yellows 848, 850, 822
Anchor Stranded Cotton: Greens
    259, 257, 269, 263

PAINTING

See the painting design on the Pull Out Pattern Sheet. See the painted background on page 9.

Follow the basic instructions as given for 'Autumn Leaves'.

The background is a much larger area to paint than for 'Autumn Leaves'. This application can be quite washy and blended. Use the techniques shown on page 6 for blending colours in washes. Remember not to paint the areas to be embroidered. Detail of the back leaves, plants and shadows can be painted in after the washy application. Keep a firm edge around the subject areas, but allow the paint to bleed and blend into the background.

EMBROIDERY

Embroider the focal point of the flowers, stems and leaves with thread painting. Pick up some of the background detail with stem stitches outlining the shapes of secondary leaves and stems.

Detail of the subtle blend of stitches in two colours of Marlitt Thread.

STENCILLING

Stencilling is a very old art form, used for centuries for decorative purposes. It has the wonderful advantage of minimum effort with maximum result. In this chapter, we will look at a simple form of stencilling on fabric which can be enhanced by beautiful embroidery.

Stencils can be made from various materials. The most common pre-cut stencils are made from paper, metal, plastic, composition products or oiled manila board. You can make your own simple stencil. Strong cartridge paper is fine for a simple stencil which will only be used once or twice.

DESIGN

To make a design for stencilling there are a few important rules to remember:

• Choose a subject which can be simplified enough to break it up into solid areas for cutting.

• It is necessary to form bridges between the cut-out areas to keep the piece together. It is preferable if these bridges form part of the design.

Your subject can be taken from many different sources. Start with sketches on paper and make simple line drawings. A good test to see if your stencil will look effective is to block out with a dark felt pen or paint the areas which will be removed. This will give you the feel for the aesthetics of the design. When you are pleased with your design, transfer it onto a piece of strong cartridge paper. A light box is good for doing this.

When you are transferring your design, make sure you leave an adequate border of paper around it to avoid accidentally getting paint onto the background fabric.

CUTTING

For cutting your stencil use a sharp blade or scalpel, and a self-healing cutting mat is a must.

Hold the blade or scalpel at an angle of 45 degrees and begin cutting, pressing firmly. Start with the smallest areas first, being careful not to cut through the bridges. If you do accidentally cut through a bridge, repair it by placing masking tape or sticky tape over both sides of the stencil and recutting the shape. Remove the cutouts as you go, cutting along the outer edge of your design line.

If possible, turn your stencil as you go, so that you are always cutting towards you, and apply smooth, steady, even pressure as you cut.

The more you do, the better you will become.

The stencil can be cut as a single image or in two or three parts which overlay one another. This will allow you to use different colours. If however, the desired effect is a subtle blended look, a single image, blending and mixing the colours as you go is far preferable.

PLACEMENT AND PAINTING

Stretch the fabric into position and tape or pin it down. Position your stencil and secure it with tape or hold it firmly over the fabric. It is important that there is no movement while you are applying the paint.

There are various ways of applying the paint – spraying, rolling, sponging or with a stencil brush. The latter is the method I prefer to use on fabric.

Stencil brushes are available in a large range of sizes, so choose one which is suitable for the size of the area you are painting.

If you are blending colours as you go, you may find it advantageous to use several different brushes – one for each colour. When using different colours in this way, it is advisable to wrap the brushes not being used at that time in a damp rag to prevent the paint drying out on the bristles.

You will notice that the ends of the bristles of a stencilling brush are flat, allowing an even application of paint. It is important that the brush be held in an upright position and that the paint is kept as dry as possible. Remember, the fabric medium you have added to your paint will make it more fluid than when it comes straight from the tube. Too much paint will result in paint bleeding under the stencil.

Do a test run before starting on your final piece. It is important to keep your edges crisp.

Once you have completed the application, remove the stencil immediately and allow the paint to dry. At this stage, you can reassess your work. This is also the ideal time to add any shading with the square shader brush. You can also incorporate a hand-painted design with the stencilling, if you desire.

Remember to heat-set your work.

I have included two very simple stencilled designs in this book. The first is a basket of embroidered flowers and the second is a simple rope design which forms a medallion on a cushion. Both these pieces feature embroidery which enhances the stencilling. These stencil designs are good for someone starting to experiment with the combination of the two mediums. Keeping it simple when you begin is always a good rule and, as you build confidence, you can progress to more advanced pieces and become more creative in your work.

In a later chapter, I have followed the stencil theme to the more advanced method of theorem painting.

BASKET OF FLOWERS

This project combines a simple stencil design with embroidery to make a beautiful basket of flowers that is suitable for framing. The three-dimensional effect of the flowers turns a basic painted area into a stunning picture.

I have used calico for this piece, however it could be enhanced even more by using a damask or self-patterned fabric.

MATERIALS

28 cm x 38 cm (11 in x 15 in) of calico

For the stencilling

Cartridge paper or, for a stronger stencil, oiled manila board or a sheet of clear Mylar

Stencil brush

Craft knife

Self-healing cutting board

Sharp HB pencil

Workboard

Masking tape

Clean white paper

Jo Sonja's Textile Medium

Jo Sonja's Artists Acrylic Gouache: Pine Green, Raw Sienna, Smoked Pearl, Paynes Gray, Rich Gold

For the embroidery

1 m (1¹/₈ yd) of 2.5 cm (1 in) wide Mokuba sheer organza ribbon, 10 Burgundy

1 m (1¹/₈ yd) of 11 mm (¹/₂ in) wide Mokuba Organdy Ribbon: 12 Cream, 14 Green, 40 Pink

2 m (2¹/₄ yd) of 5 mm (¹/₄ in) wide Mokuba Organdy Ribbon, 15 Green

1 m (1¹/₈ yd) of 11 mm (¹/₂ in) wide Mokuba Rayon Ribbon, 40 Pink

1 m (1¹/₈ yd) of 11 mm (¹/₂ in) wide Mokuba Luminous Ribbon 4599, 14 Burgundy/Green

50 cm (20 in) of 11 mm (¹/₂ in) wide Mokuba Variegated Ribbon 4882, 1 Cream/Green

3 m (3¹/₂ yd) of Cotton on Creations, Chenille: Chiffon or Copper Mauve

Anchor Marlitt Rayon Thread, Gold 1078

Anchor Stranded Cotton, Pink 969

Chenille needles

STENCILLING

See the stencil design on page 22.

STEP ONE

Trace the stencil design onto the stencil material and cut it out. Tape the calico over the white paper onto the work surface.

STEP TWO

Mix small amounts of Pine Green, Raw Sienna, Smoked Pearl and a touch of Paynes Gray to make a smoky green colour. Mix in the textile medium. Tape the stencil in place and, using the stencil brush, apply this colour.

STEP THREE

Brush Rich Gold lightly over the painted area, following the direction of the fabric weave.

A simple stencil design combines beautifully with embroidery.

EMBROIDERY

See the embroidery design on page 24.

Note: The numbers in brackets below correspond to the numbers on the embroidery design. Use these as a guide for placement.

STEP ONE

Using the sharp pencil, transfer the basket grid (1) from the pattern over the top of the painted basket. Using the chenille thread, work a large stem stitch over the grid lines in one direction across the basket. Weave the thread back in the opposite direction to form a basketweave (2). Anchor the thread by pulling the needle through to the back of the fabric.

STEP TWO

Using the wide Burgundy organza ribbon, stitch in the bows (3) on the basket handle and rim.

STEP THREE

Make five ribbon roses (4) using the 11 mm ($\frac{1}{2}$ in) wide Pink rayon ribbon and secure them in place, working from the back of the fabric and using an ordinary sewing thread.

STEP FOUR

Using the sheer Burgundy ribbon and ribbon stitch, create the open roses (5). Work French knots at the top of the stamens, which are worked in the Gold Marlitt thread.

STEP FIVE

Scatter groups of open rose petals using the 11 mm ($\frac{1}{2}$ in) wide Cream (6) and Pink (7) organdy ribbons.

STEP SIX

Using the Anchor Stranded Cotton, work French knots (8) indicating the centres for the sheer petals. Using the same thread, work scattered French knots in groups of three for buds.

STEP SEVEN

Using the variegated ribbon and ribbon stitch, make larger petals as fillers in the design (11). Work leaves in groups of three, in ribbon stitch, using the wider Green organdy ribbon for the larger leaves (9) and the narrower Green organdy ribbon for the smaller ones (10).

MAKING UP

Have your finished picture professionally framed. Ask your framer to pad slightly behind the fabric to give it extra loft. The picture can be framed with or without glass.

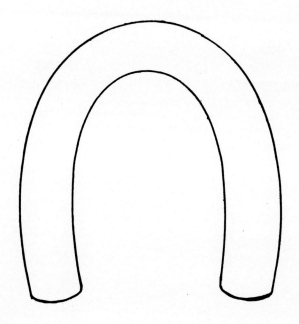

STENCIL DESIGN

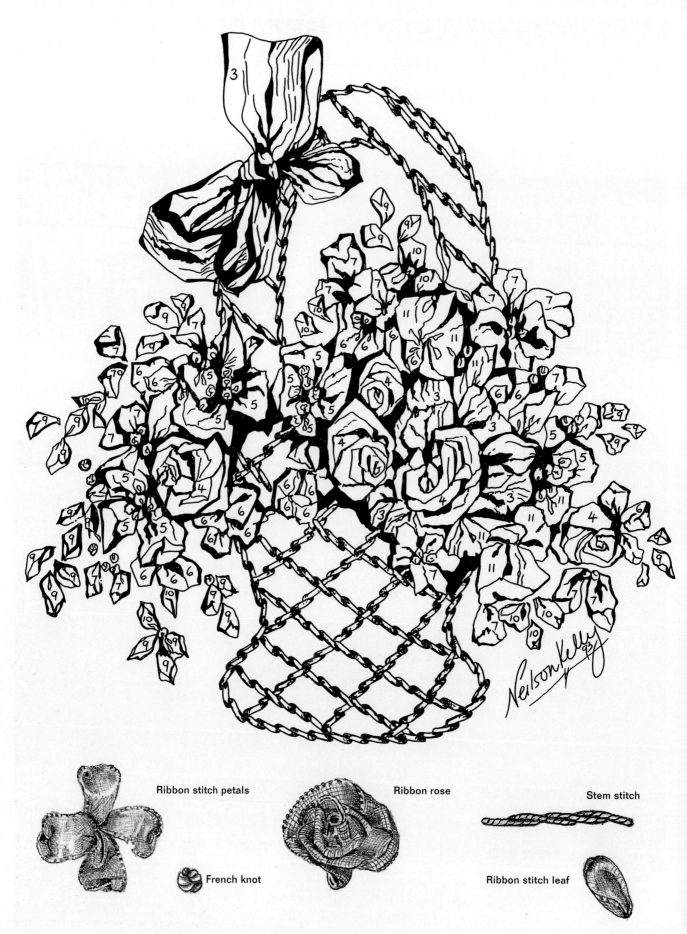

Ribbon stitch petals

Ribbon rose

Stem stitch

French knot

Ribbon stitch leaf

EMBROIDERY DESIGN AND KEY

24

CALICO HEART

This heart-shaped medallion cushion has a simple stencilled design which is enhanced with ribbon embroidery. It would also be suitable for framing, or the design could be reduced and used on the flap of a lingerie bag with a tassel at the peak.

MATERIALS

For the stencilling
38 cm (15 in) square of calico
Cartridge paper or, for a stronger stencil, oiled manila board or a sheet of clear Mylar
Stencil brush
Craft knife
Self-healing cutting board
HB pencil
Workboard
Masking tape
Clean white paper
Jo Sonja's Textile Medium
Jo Sonja's Artists Acrylic Gouache: Pine Green, Burgundy

For the embroidery
50 cm (20 in) of Mokuba Rayon Ribbon 1505, 12 Cream
1 m (1¹/₈ yd) of 13 mm (¹/₂ in) wide Mokuba Luminous Ribbon 4599, 15 Burgundy/Blue
2 m (2¹/₄ yd) of 5 mm (¹/₄ in) wide Mokuba Organdy Ribbon 1500, 16 Dark Green
50 cm (20 in) of 15 mm (⁵/₈ in) wide Mokuba Crepe Georgette 4546, 29 Dusty Pink
50 cm (20 in) each of 11 mm (¹/₂ in) wide Mokuba Organdy Ribbon 1500: 12 Cream, 40 Pink
Anchor Marlitt Rayon Thread: Gold 1078, Green 826
Anchor Stranded Cotton, Pink 969
Chenille needles
Scissors

STENCILLING

See the stencil design on page 29.

___

STEP ONE

Trace the stencil design onto the stencil material and cut it out. Tape the piece of calico over the white paper, onto the workboard.

___

STEP TWO

Pick up a small amount of Pine Green and Burgundy on the same brush. The application of the paint in this design is very dry and shaded, with the darker area on the inner edge of the ribbon.

EMBROIDERY

See the embroidery design and key on pages 28–29.
Note: The numbers in brackets in the instructions correspond to the numbers on the embroidery design. Use these as a guide for placement.

___

STEP ONE

Make two ribbon roses from the Cream rayon ribbon and attach them at the points indicated (1).

Hand-made roses and ribbon embroidery add another dimension.

STEP TWO

Work open roses in ribbon stitch, using the Burgundy ribbon (2). The open roses help to form the crown at the top of the medallion, as well as making the peak at the bottom. For the centre of the roses, work French knots in the Green Marlitt thread.

STEP THREE

Work the large petals at the side in ribbon stitch, using the Dusty Pink georgette ribbon (3).

STEP FOUR

Using ribbon stitch, add extra petals for the open roses in 11 mm ($^1/_2$ in) wide Cream (4) and Pink (5) ribbon.

STEP FIVE

Work the petals on both sides of the embroidered areas, using the chenille thread and lazy daisy stitch (6). Work French knots for the centres in the Gold Marlitt thread.

STEP SIX

Work the leaves in lazy daisy stitch in the Dark Green organdy ribbon. Scatter French knots in the Pink stranded cotton to indicate buds.

MAKING UP

Have your cushion made up professionally or make it up yourself, following the general instructions for making cushions on page 8.

Ribbon that is stitched in makes beautiful flowers with French knot centres.

EMBROIDERY DESIGN

STENCIL DESIGN

 Ribbon rose

 Ribbon stitch petals

 French knot

 Fly stitch

 Ribbon stitch leaf

 Lazy daisy stitch

EMBROIDERY KEY

THEOREM PAINTING

**Theorem painting is an old technique that like so many
wonderful traditional arts, has experienced a revival in recent times.**

Traditionally, theorem painting was done on velvet, so we often think of the process as painting on velvet. However, the word 'theorem' actually relates to the stencil process, rather than the fabric it is painted on. Theorem painting can be done on many different surfaces.

Theorem painting was used extensively in ancient China. It is most commonly known as a Victorian art, but was well documented in early American settlement. Early pieces of theorem painting are very valuable and extremely hard to come by.

It is an art form which is achievable by most people, as the painting is done through a series of stencils which, when overlaid and combined with beautiful shading, highlights and depths, can create an almost hand-painted look.

It is an ideal technique for making glorious cushions and framed pieces, and you can enhance them even more by adding touches of beautiful embroidery and beading.

In this book, I have included theorem designs in two different themes – cherubs and flowers. There are two divine cherub cushions with embroidered trailing garlands of roses, as well as an angel in flight, inspired by ancient etchings. The floral theme features a wonderful pansy cushion with strong colours and a beautiful pansy pincushion in warm sienna colours for your sewing table or those special collectable hat pins. Finally, there is a lush rose design painted to frame or for a box lid.

THE THEOREM PROCESS

STEP ONE

Photocopy the design once onto the Mylar sheet.

STEP TWO

Place the image on the film, face up on the photocopier. Print the next five sheets of film as a reverse image – the ink side of the copy should be underneath the design when it is held with the correct side of the design facing up.

STEP THREE

Seal the underside of the stencil with shellac so that the photocopy ink doesn't transfer to the velvet during painting. This is very important.

STEP FOUR

Number the stencil sheets 1–5. Cut the stencils, cutting only the areas numbered for that stencil sheet; for example, cut all the areas marked (1) on the sheet marked (1) and so forth.

STEP FIVE

Back the piece of velvet with a piece of Contact adhesive plastic the same size as the velvet. This will keep the fabric flat and taut, while you paint. Place the backed fabric on to the workboard.

STEP SIX

Place the first stencil into position on the fabric. It is not necessary to tape the stencils to the fabric. Flexibility of movement is essential.

STEP SEVEN

Make up your palette with the oil colours needed for the piece. Only small amounts of paint are needed at a time. Remember, oil paints can get very messy, so try to keep the palette clean while working. Use a separate piece of rag or a separate brush for each colour.

STEP EIGHT

The paint can be applied with a stiff brush or with a rag wrapped around your index finger or a combination of both methods. It is a good idea to do a bit of experimenting with application and shading before attempting the final piece. Choose a largish area to start with, so you have the opportunity to vary the shading. Leave strong highlighted areas without paint, softly blending the lighter shades in a slightly circular motion, working with the grain of the fabric, then build up depth areas for the shadows with the deeper colours. You will need to evaluate the design before you start, so that you are aware of the individual sections, in order to make sure that all the petals of a rose are painted pink and the leaves are painted green. With stencils, it is sometimes easy to get confused.

STEP NINE

Continue to work through the design, overlaying each stencil in turn to form another section of the design. When you have worked your way through all the stencils, you may need to go back to work on some areas that don't meet up. Do this by simply overlaying the appropriate stencil and moving it into a position that will allow those areas to meet properly.

STEP TEN

Using a fine liner brush and thinning the paint with a small amount of turps, paint in any fine detail, such as the eyes on a face or the veins on a leaf.

STEP ELEVEN

When you have completed the painting, it is necessary to allow the oil paints to dry completely. This can take anything up to a week, depending on the thickness of the paint application and the weather.

STEP TWELVE

Once the oils are completely dry, it is time to prepare the dye – the velvet can be dyed in either tea or coffee for an aged look. Make the dye solutions very weak to very strong, depending on the overall look that you wish to achieve. Make the dye just as you would prepare a cup of tea or coffee. Keep in mind the size of the fabric to be dyed, as this will determine the quantity of dye needed. Immerse the fabric in the dye solution until the desired effect is achieved.

STEP THIRTEEN

Do not hang the velvet up to dry. The fabric can be dried in two ways. In the first method, it can be scrunched up when it is taken out of the dye, removing a lot of the wetness and also some of the colour. This effect is fabulous for an aged, crunched look, and there will be a variation in the colours of the dye. Spread it out on a towel and dry it flat.

The second method is to dip the fabric into the dye solution and lay it out flat on a towel immediately, without scrunching. This will keep the all-over colour of the dyeing even.

STEP FOURTEEN

Now is the time to add any embellishment or embroidery, then your piece is ready to make up or to frame.

PANSY CUSHION

Pansies are the most wonderful little flowers and conjure up thoughts of happiness. Traditionally, the pansy is the flower of thought, remembrance and friendship.

This cushion has a wonderful all-over design featuring bright, deep colours. It has been dyed in coffee for an antique look, and trimmed with stunning onion braid. The pansies would also be beautiful with a subtle embellishment of beading in the centre of the flowers.

MATERIALS

38 cm (15 in) square of cream cotton velvet for the front
38 cm (15 in) square of Contact adhesive plastic
Six sheets of clear Mylar
Workboard
Winsor & Newton Artists Oil Colours: Olive, Sap Green, Black, Cadmium Yellow, Cadmium Red, Cobalt Blue, French Ultramarine, Alizarin Crimson, Raw Sienna, Burnt Sienna, Diox Purple
Shellac
Mineral turps
Soft, old rags for the paint application
Craft knife and blade
Self-healing cutting mat
Palette (a milk carton, cleaned and cut flat, is fine)
Short-haired liner brush or a size 0 round brush

PREPARATION

See the painting design on the Pull Out Pattern Sheet.

Note: This design uses five stencils. Follow the instructions on pages 20, 30 and 31 for preparation of the stencils and fabric.

Prepare the five stencils as instructed and number them 1–5. Prepare the square of velvet and place it on the workboard with the nap coming towards you.

PAINTING

STEP ONE

I have used a combination of the following colours for the petals – Cobalt Blue, French Ultramarine, Alizarin Crimson, Raw Sienna, Burnt Sienna, Diox Purple. The colours are applied with a rag wrapped around the finger. The leaves are painted in Olive and Sap Green.

Leave areas of highlights and create depth behind the petals.

STEP TWO

Use Black shaded into the centre of the pansies, Cadmium Yellow for the centre with Cadmium Red for the tiny tongue in the middle.

STEP THREE

Hand-paint the centre detail with the fine line brush. You can add extra detail of veins to leaves and petals if you want to, but it is not necessary if your shading is well applied.

STEP FOUR

When the painting is completed and the piece is thoroughly dry, immerse it in a strong solution of coffee. Remember, if it is too dark, you can always wash some of the colour out with clean water.

MAKING UP

This cushion has been professionally made up. You can make up your own cushion, following the instructions on page 8. The piece would look equally beautiful in an ornate frame.

ROSE BOX

**The roses in this project are double-shaded to give them extra depth and warmth.
The base colours are painted and shaded to completion, then the stencils are
re-laid and a final colour is blended over the top.**

This piece has been framed as a pad-ded top in the recess of a box lid, however, it could just as easily be used to make a gorgeous lingerie bag or a framed picture.

MATERIALS

Suitable box with an insert lid
Piece of wadding for padding
26 cm x 36 cm (10¼ in x 14¼ in) of cream cotton velvet
26 cm x 36 cm (10¼ in x 14¼ in) of Contact adhesive plastic
Six sheets of clear Mylar
Winsor & Newton Artists Oil Colours: Cadmium Yellow Hue, Raw Sienna, Alizarin Crimson, Olive, Titanium White
Shellac
Mineral turps
Soft, old rags for the paint application
Craft knife and blade
Self-healing cutting mat
Palette (a milk carton, cleaned and cut flat, is fine)
Short-haired liner brush or a size 0 round brush

PREPARATION

See the painting design on page 36.

Note: This piece uses five stencils. Follow the instructions on pages 30–31 for preparation of the stencils and fab-ric, and the process of application.
    Prepare the five stencils as in-structed and number them 1–5. Pre-pare the square of velvet and place it on the work surface with the nap coming towards you.

PAINTING

Note: The paint is applied with a soft rag, wrapped around the index finger, instead of a brush.

STEP ONE

For the rose petals, I have blended a combination of Cadmium Yellow Hue and Raw Sienna as a base, then shaded heavily over the top with Alizarin Crimson, with shadow areas in Olive. In the final blend, add a touch of Tita-nium White with the Alizarin Crimson on the turn backs of the roses.

STEP TWO

For the leaves, calyx and stems, use Olive with a tint of Alizarin Crimson.

STEP THREE

When the theorem process is completed, join the leaves and paint a suggestion of veins in the leaves with the fine liner brush.

MAKING UP

Make up the box lid, inserting the painted velvet panel.
Note: This box has a painted tortoise-shell finish. For detailed technical instructions for creating this finish, see my first book in this series *Creative Inspirations in Paint*. The box could be simply lacquered, antiqued or gilded.

Double-shade the rose for extra depth and warmth.

PAINTING DESIGN

36

PANSY PINCUSHION

This dear little pincushion features an all-over design similar
to the one on the pansy cushion on page 32.

MATERIALS

38 cm (15 in) square of cream
  cotton velvet
38 cm (15 in) square of Contact
  adhesive plastic
Six sheets of Mylar
Winsor & Newton Artists Oil
  Colours: Yellow Hue, Cadmium
  Yellow, Burnt Sienna, Olive
Acrylic paint, Black
Water-based varnish
Shellac
Mineral turps
Soft, old rags for the paint application
Craft knife and blade
Self-healing cutting mat
Palette (a milk carton, cleaned and
  cut flat, is fine)
Short-haired liner brush or a size 0
  round brush
Round wooden cushion base, 15 cm
  (6 in) diameter
Braid
Paints, stain or gilding materials –
  depending on the finish required
  for the wooden base

PREPARATION

See the stencil design on page 38.

Note: This design uses five stencils.
Follow the instructions on pages 30–31
for preparation of the stencils and
fabric, and the process of application.

Prepare the five stencils as instructed and number them 1–5.
Prepare the square of velvet and place
it on the work surface with the nap
coming towards you.

**Pansies blended in warm tones of siennas
and yellows and dyed in coffee.**

PAINTING

STEP ONE

I have used Yellow Hue, Cadmium
Yellow and Burnt Sienna, shaded and
blended together, for the petals. The
leaves and background are Olive.

STEP TWO

When all the painting is completed
and the piece is completely dry, dye it
in strong coffee.

MAKING UP

STEP ONE

I painted the wooden base with Black
acrylic paint before it was gilded.
Splits in the gilding sheets have
assured that the Black will show
through for an antique look. Seal the
gilding with the water-based varnish.

STEP TWO

Have your pincushion professionally
upholstered, adding a braid trim.

STENCIL DESIGN

DIVINE CHERUBS

These divine cherub cushions have been tea-dyed and trimmed with a gorgeous tassel braid. They could just as easily be mounted in an opulent gold frame.

I have painted the drapery with a combination of blues, but you can select your own colour scheme.

MATERIALS

For each cushion
Two 38 cm (15 in) squares of cream cotton velvet for each cushion
For the painting
38 cm (15 in) square of Contact adhesive plastic
Six sheets of clear Mylar
Workboard
Winsor & Newton Artists Oil Colours: Raw Sienna, Burnt Sienna, Cobalt Blue, Cerulean Blue, French Ultramarine, Olive, Flesh, Cadmium Red, Viridian Hue, Warm White
Shellac
Mineral turps
Soft, old rags for the paint application
Craft knife and blade
Self-healing cutting mat
Palette (a milk carton, cleaned and cut flat, is fine)
Short-haired liner brush or a size 0 round brush
For the embroidery
Watercolours Variegated Threads
Chenille needle

PREPARATION

See the painting designs on the Pull Out Pattern Sheet and the embroidery designs and key on pages 42-43.

Note: These theorem cherubs use five stencils each.
Prepare the five stencils as instructed on pages 30–31 and number

them 1–5. Prepare the square of velvet and place it on the workboard with the nap coming towards you.

PAINTING

STEP ONE

Place the first stencil onto the velvet and begin painting. The hair is painted in a combination of Raw Sienna and Burnt Sienna. The drape is painted in a shading of Cobalt Blue, Cerulean Blue and French Ultramarine, with touches of Olive and Burnt Sienna for depth. The mandolin and bow and arrow have been painted with a combination of Raw Sienna and Burnt Sienna. The skin tone is a soft application of Flesh, with a touch of Burnt Sienna. The lips are Cadmium Red. The wings are a combination of the Viridian Hue, mixed with a little Warm White, with a touch of Cerulean Blue and Olive for depth.

STEP TWO

When all the stencils are completed, paint in the details, such as the

Use a liner brush to paint in the detail on the cherub's face.

mandolin strings, using the liner brush. Carefully hand-paint the eyes and nostrils with Burnt Sienna, using the liner brush. Use a small amount of turps to thin the oils so that you can create a fine line. Practise your fine lines on a piece of scrap fabric first.

EMBELLISHING

The trail of roses has been embroidered in a variegated thread from the Watercolour range and features rosettes, French knots and lazy daisy stitches. There are some wonderful colour combinations available in variegated threads, so choose the one which complements the colours of your painting.

Embroider the flowers using the key on page 43 and referring to the stitch guide on pages 76–78.

MAKING UP

Have your cushions made up prefessionally or do it yourself, following the instructions on page 8.

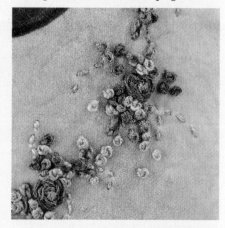
French knots, rosettes and lazy daisy stitches make a lovely garland.

41

EMBROIDERY DESIGN

KEY

Thread rosette

Straight stitch

Lazy daisy stitch

French knot

EMBROIDERY DESIGN

43

ANGEL OF ROSES

This flying angel was inspired by an ancient etching. The colours I've used are a mixture of earthy tones and heavenly colours for the wings. The piece is ideal for framing, covering a box lid or for making a stunning cushion.

The roses carried by the angel have been embroidered with silk ribbons and variegated threads, after the piece was coffee-dyed. I have chosen a beautifully ornate frame for this piece, giving it a very special feel.

MATERIALS

36 cm x 48 cm (14 in x 19 in) of
  cream cotton velvet
For the painting
36 cm x 48 cm (14 in x 19 in) of
  Contact adhesive plastic
Six sheets of clear Mylar
Workboard
Winsor & Newton Artists Oil Colours:
  Burnt Sienna, Raw Sienna, Olive,
  Viridian Hue, Warm White, Flesh,
  Cadmium Red
Shellac
Mineral turps
Soft, old rags for the paint application
Craft knife and blade
Self-healing cutting mat
Palette (a milk carton, cleaned and
  cut flat, is fine)
Short-haired liner brush or a size 0
  round brush
For the embroidery
Chenille needles
Petals Hand-dyed Silk Ribbon:
  Country Sunflower, Cafe Mocha,
  Brown Sugar, Rose Gold
Watercolours Variegated Threads,
  Antique Brass 128
Needles Necessities Overdyed Floss
  Colour 128

PREPARATION

See the painting design on the Pull Out Pattern Sheet.

Note: This angel uses five stencils. Follow the instructions on pages 30–31 for preparation of the stencils and fabric, and the process of application.

Prepare the five stencils as instructed and number them 1–5. Prepare the square of velvet and place it on the workboard with the nap coming towards you.

PAINTING

STEP ONE

Place the first stencil onto the velvet and begin painting. Use a combination, blending Burnt Sienna, Raw Sienna and Olive for the dress and drapery. The wings are Viridian Hue mixed with Warm White and Raw Sienna. Use Flesh and Burnt Sienna for the skin, Burnt Sienna for the eyes and a subtle indication of the nostrils. The lips are Cadmium Red. The hair is a very light blend of Raw Sienna with a touch of Burnt Sienna at the base. Paint the details on the face using the liner brush: the lips are Cadmium Red; the eyes, eyebrows and nostrils are Burnt Sienna.

EMBROIDERY

See the embroidery design and key on page 46.

I have used beautiful variegated silk ribbons in soft subtle colours, and variegated threads to embroider the bundle of trailing roses. Embroider the flowers referring to the stitch guide on pages 76–78.

STEP ONE

Work the ribbon rosettes in the colours listed, scattering them throughout the design. Work the thread rosettes in the variegated thread.

STEP TWO

The leaves are lazy daisy stitch worked in Antique Brass with a few straight stitches to extend the design.

STEP THREE

Embroider the random, scattered buds in French knots, using both silk ribbon and thread. The French knots can also be used as a filler to make an area more dense, then trail out loosely.

Rosettes are stitched in hand-dyed ribbon.

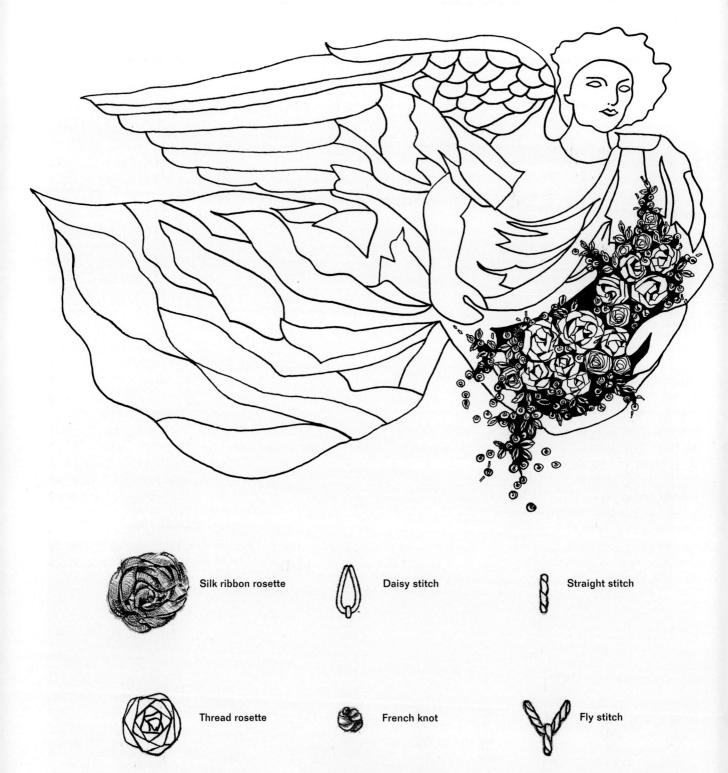

Silk ribbon rosette

Daisy stitch

Straight stitch

Thread rosette

French knot

Fly stitch

EMBROIDERY DESIGN AND KEY

FACES AND CHERUBS

In this section, we look at painting faces, bodies and skin tones for decorative purposes. Of course, it is not possible to give full life drawing and painting instructions in this chapter, but I will give you some useful hints.

The first things to consider when approaching the painting of your subject is the basic shape and direction of the face, body or limb. If you are painting from life, check the proportions of each part to the others. Consider the contours, musculature and bone. Note the light direction and the shadows.

These are a few basic matters to keep in mind before you start:

• You can paint freehand or transfer the basic shape from a picture or photograph. Usually, the best observation is from life, but a photograph or even a picture from a magazine is probably more suitable for this purpose, so that you can experiment – observing and painting what you see. This is a really helpful exercise.

• When choosing colours for skin tones, it is important not to make your painting too orange or too pink. This seems to be one of the most common mistakes I see. I always advise my students when painting on fabric to start with a neutral colour, then build up contours with skin-tone colours. For example, the basic shape of the face or body could be painted with Jo Sonja's Artists Acrylic Gouache, Smoked Pearl. A skin-tone colour such as Blush could then be used to start shaping the contours of the chin, nose, forehead etc, after which shadowed areas around the hairline, eyes, nose, chin, neck and ears can be added with Burnt Sienna. Use a shaded load of colour when painting.

• Deeper colour can be brought in for sharper and more defined shadows around the nostrils, folds in the eyelids, mouth and so on.

• Pink or peach colours can be used to blush colour onto the cheeks and also reflect into the chin and forehead area.

• A deeper colour can be used for painting in the lips.

Shadows, light areas and highlights are the most important aspects of your work as they will give your painting lifelike contours.

• When we look at highlights, the ideal example is, of course, the eye. It is the highlight in the eye that gives it life and direction. Even if you are painting very basic eyes, that little white dot, inside the bigger dark dot – so to speak – will give it life. One word of caution – make sure that both highlights are facing in the same direction. There is nothing worse than making your masterpiece cross-eyed.

• When painting a figure or face which will later be embroidered, consider the areas that will be embellished. A light box can be useful for transferring the placement marks for the embroidery, after your painting is completed. Remember to heat-set the paint before you begin embroidering.

On the following pages, I will show you some of my favourite pieces. I hope you will try them for yourself.

Think how lovely it would be if you were to paint a member of your family or the face of a child, and embroider a garland of flowers in her hair.

ANASTASIA

This angelic face conjures up images of contemplation and reminiscence – a special design for an area of relaxation and serenity. The garland in her hair is embroidered in soft, subtle colours in threads and ribbons. The cushion has an old-fashioned feel and features luxurious fringing, but it would look just as lovely in a gilded frame.

MATERIALS

38 cm (15 in) square of ivory moiré taffeta for the front

For the painting

$1/2$" square shader brush
$1/4$" square shader brush
Liner brush, size 0
Jar of water
Palette (a milk carton, cleaned and flattened, is fine)
Sharp HB pencil
Light box (optional)
Workboard
Masking tape
Clean white paper
Jo Sonja's Textile Medium
Jo Sonja's Artists Acrylic Gouache: Smoked Pearl, Burnt Sienna, Raw Sienna, Burgundy, Titanium White
Jo Sonja's Traditional European Background Colour, Blush

For the embroidery

Chenille needles, various sizes
Water-soluble marker pen
Mokuba Rayon Ribbon, 12 Cream, for large flowers
4 mm ($3/16$ in) wide YLI Silk Ribbon, 156 Cream
Paterna Stranded Wool: Cream 262, Blue/grey 392, Green 642
Anchor Stranded Cotton: Pink 778, Green 681

PREPARATION

See the painting, the embroidery design and key on page 51.

STEP ONE

Using the pencil, lightly transfer the design to the fabric. A light box can make this easier. If you don't have a light box, tape the design to a window with the light coming through it. Tape the fabric over the top and trace the design. Place the fabric over the clean white paper and tape it down on the workboard.

STEP TWO

Prepare the palette, mixing the fabric medium with the paints following the manufacturer's instructions.

PAINTING

STEP ONE

Using the $1/2$" brush, start with Smoked Pearl as the base colour for the skin tone and gently blend in touches of Blush, with Burnt Sienna, to create the contours and shadows of the face. Pay particular attention to the shadow areas around the eyes, under the hairline and under the chin. Shade out the colour from the neck area into the fabric colour.

STEP TWO

Paint in the eyes, eyelids and eyebrows with Burnt Sienna using the liner brush. Don't forget to paint the highlight in the eyes with a dash of Titanium White.

STEP THREE

Paint the lips in Blush, lined gently with a touch of Burnt Sienna added to the Blush, to give a stronger line.

STEP FOUR

Paint the hair, using the $1/2$" brush and a combination of Smoked Pearl, a touch of Raw Sienna and Burnt Sienna. Make waves in the application, giving a soft, flowing appearance.

STEP FIVE

Remove the paper from the back of the fabric so that it doesn't stick when the paint dries. Allow the painting to dry completely, then heat-set it by ironing on the back of the fabric.

Paint shadows and highlights to contour the face.

49

EMBROIDERY

STEP ONE

Transfer the embroidery design of the circlet to the painted cherub, using the water-soluble pen or the pencil. Again, a light box is handy for this process as it allows you to see through the fabric to the design underneath. Alternatively, you can mark only the direction lines for the embroidery and design your own placement.

STEP TWO

Embroider the circlet, using the placement design and key, and referring to the stitch guide on pages 76–78. Begin with the large flowers in ribbon stitch, using the rayon ribbon. Work a French knot in the centre of this flower, using the same rayon ribbon.

STEP THREE

Work the straight stitch daisy in 262, the rosettes in silk ribbon and in stranded cotton 778. Use the same colour for the bullion flowers and buds. Embroider the leaves last, using green wool and cotton.

MAKING UP

This cushion has been made up professionally. You could make up the cushion yourself, following the general instructions for cushions on page 8. The piece would look equally good, if it was framed as a picture.

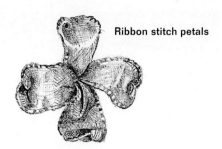 Ribbon stitch petals

 Fly stitch

 Ribbon stitch leaves

 French knot

 Bullion stitch

 Straight stitch

 Blanket stitch flower

 Silk ribbon rosette

 Thread rosette

 Lazy daisy stitch

EMBROIDERY KEY

A combination of threads, ribbons and textures makes a beautiful circlet.

PAINTING AND EMBROIDERY
DESIGN

CLAUDIA

Named after a special friend, this framed painting of a beautiful lady has a painted rose swag across her shoulders and an embroidered hair garland. Various stitches, threads and ribbons have been used to give depth and texture to the piece.

MATERIALS

38 cm (15 in) square of ivory moiré taffeta for the front

For the painting

¹/₂" square shader brush
¹/₄" square shader brush
Liner brush, size 0
Jar of water
Palette (a milk carton, cleaned and flattened, is fine)
Sharp HB pencil
Light box (optional)
Workboard
Masking tape
Clean white paper
Jo Sonja's Textile Medium
Jo Sonja's Artists Acrylic Gouache: Smoked Pearl, Burnt Sienna, Raw Sienna, Burgundy, Titanium White, Paynes Gray, Black, Blush, Pine Green, Teal Green

For the embroidery

Chenille needles
Water-soluble marker pen
4 mm (³/₁₆ in) wide YLI Silk Ribbon: 158, 162, 163 Pinks; 156 Cream
Paterna Stranded Wool: Pink 924, Flesh 494, Cream 262
Anchor Stranded Cotton: Pinks 895, 893; Cream 926; Green 845; Blue 161; Yellow 300

PREPARATION

See the painting and embroidery design and key on page 55.

STEP ONE

Using the pencil, lightly transfer the design to the fabric. A light box can make this easier. See page 7 for the use of the light box and an alternative. Place the fabric over the sheet of clean white paper and tape it down on the workboard.

STEP TWO

Prepare the palette, mixing the fabric medium with the paints following the manufacturer's instructions.

PAINTING

STEP ONE

Using the ¹/₂" brush, start with Smoked Pearl as the base colour for the skin tone and gently blend in touches of Blush with Burnt Sienna to create the contours and shadows of the face. Pay particular attention to the shadow

Give life to the eyes with strong highlights.

52

areas around the eyes, under the hair-line and under the chin. Shade out the colour from the neck area into the fabric colour.

STEP TWO

Paint the iris of the eye in Paynes Gray, then lighten the Paynes Gray by adding varying amounts of Smoked Pearl. The pupil, eye line and lashes are painted in Black, using the liner brush. The eyelids and eyebrows are painted with Burnt Sienna using the liner brush. Feather in the eyebrows so as not to get a hard line. Don't forget to paint the highlight in the eyes with a dash of Titanium White.

STEP THREE

Paint the lips in Blush, with a touch of Burgundy. Gently line the lips with a touch of Burnt Sienna added to the Blush to give a stronger line.

STEP FOUR

Paint the hair using the $^1/_2$" brush and a combination of Smoked Pearl, a touch of Raw Sienna and Burnt Sienna. Make waves in the application, giving a soft, flowing appearance.

STEP FIVE

Paint the roses in Smoked Pearl for the light-value colour, Burgundy mixed with Smoked Pearl and a touch of Raw Sienna for the mid-value colour and Burgundy for the deep-value colour.

The buds and leaves are painted with Smoked Pearl, Pine Green and Teal Green.

STEP SIX

Remove the paper from the back of the fabric so that it doesn't stick when the paint dries. Allow the painting to dry completely, then heat-set it by ironing on the back of the fabric.

Combine threads and silk ribbon for a richly textured effect.

EMBROIDERY

STEP ONE

Transfer the embroidery design of the garland to the painted face, using the water-soluble pen. Again, a light box is handy for this process as it allows you to see through the fabric to the design underneath. Alternatively, you can mark only the direction lines for the embroidery and design your own placement for the flowers.

STEP TWO

Embroider the circlet, using the placement design and key, and referring to the stitch guide on pages 76–78. This garland is worked in four main groups across her hair; stitch the central flowers of each group first and take care to maintain the varying thicknesses. Embroider the rosettes in all the colours of the silk ribbon and the stranded wool 924 and 494. Use stranded wool 262 for the straight stitch daisies, with centres in stranded cotton 300. For the bullion flowers and buds, use stranded cotton 893 and 895. Embroider the gypsophila in stranded cotton 926 and the forget-me-nots in stranded cotton 161.

STEP THREE

Embroider the leaves, calyx and stems in stranded cotton 845.

Scatter additional flowers around this circlet as you wish – please don't think it is necessary to stick rigidly to my design.

MAKING UP

Have your picture professionally framed. It's a good idea to ask your framer to put a little wadding behind the picture to give it extra loft.

Straight stitch daisy

Silk ribbon rosette

Bullion stitch

Fly stitch

Silk ribbon rosette

French knot

Lazy daisy stitch

PAINTING AND EMBROIDERY
DESIGN AND KEY

VALENTINE CHERUB

This lovely cushion could be used as a brooch cushion or as a centre-piece against the pillows on a beautiful bed. Whatever use you find for this design, it will add a touch of romance to your surroundings.

MATERIALS

38 cm (15 in) square of ivory moiré taffeta for the front

For the painting
$^1/_2$" square shader brush
$^1/_4$" square shader brush
Liner brush, size 00
Jar of water
Palette (a milk carton, cleaned and flattened, is fine)
Sharp HB pencil
Light box (optional)
Workboard
Masking tape
Clean white paper
Jo Sonja's Textile Medium
Jo Sonja's Artists Acrylic Gouache: Smoked Pearl, Burnt Sienna, Raw Sienna, Burgundy, Titanium White, Teal Green, Paynes Gray, Pine Green
Jo Sonja's European Background Colour, Blush

For the embroidery
Chenille needles, various sizes
Beading needle
Water-soluble marker pen
Small pearls
4 mm ($^3/_{16}$ in) wide YLI Silk Ribbon: 158, 160 Pinks; 131 Blue
Anchor Marlitt Rayon Thread: 827 Green, 1212 Cream

PREPARATION

See the painting and embroidery design and key on page 59.

STEP ONE

Using the pencil, lightly transfer the design to the fabric. A light box can make this easier. See page 7 for the use of the light box and an alternative. Place the fabric over a sheet of clean white paper and tape it down on the workboard.

STEP TWO

Prepare the palette, mixing the fabric medium with the paints following the manufacturer's instructions.

PAINTING

STEP ONE

Using the $^1/_2$" brush, start with Smoked Pearl as the base colour for the skin tone and gently blend in touches of Blush with Burnt Sienna to create the contours and shadows of the face.

Pearls and silk ribbon embroidery add a romantic touch.

Paint in the eyes, eyelids and eyebrows with Burnt Sienna, using the liner brush. Paint the lips in Burgundy.

STEP TWO

Paint the hair, using the 1/4" brush, in a combination of Smoked Pearl and a touch of Raw Sienna and Burnt Sienna.

STEP THREE

Paint the roses, using Smoked Pearl as the light-value colour, Burgundy mixed with Smoked Pearl and a touch of Raw Sienna for the mid-value colour and Burgundy for the deep-value colour. Extensions of the buds and leaves are painted with Smoked Pearl, Pine Green and Teal Green.

STEP FOUR

Paint the wings in a mixture of Teal Green and Titanium White, with a touch of Paynes Gray.

STEP FIVE

Remove the paper from the back of the fabric so that it doesn't stick when the paint dries. Allow the painting to dry completely, then heat-set it by ironing on the back of the fabric.

EMBROIDERY

STEP ONE

Transfer the embroidery design of the garland onto the painted cherub, using the water-soluble pen. Again, a light box is handy for this process as it allows you to see through the fabric to the design underneath. Alternatively, you can mark only the direction of the lines for the embroidery and design your own placement for the flowers.

STEP TWO

Embroider the flowers, using the design and key, and referring to the stitch guide on pages 76–78. Work silk ribbon rosettes in 158 and extra petals in ribbon stitch in 158 and 160. Add forget-me-nots in 131. Work calyx, leaves and stems in 827 and buds in 1212. Trail leaves, petals and buds around the vine as indicated.

STEP THREE

Using the beading needle, sew on the small pearls, scattering them through the circlet and garland.

MAKING UP

This cushion has been professionally made up. You can make up your own cushion, following the general instructions on page 8.

Hand-painted baby roses add to the romantic feel.

KEY

Stem stitch

French knot

Ribbon stitch leaf

PAINTING AND
EMBROIDERY DESIGN

FLYING CHERUBS

This gorgeous cherub fabric inspired me to paint the actual woven cherub design, making a central feature to embroider. Colour tinting fabric is an interesting exercise and can be done with many fabrics and many subjects.

The cherub design is copyright to the manufacturer, as with any design on a purchased fabric. However, I am including the colours for painting and the embroidery instructions, which are suitable for any other cherub design you may find on any other fabric. This piece has been framed but would be just as lovely made into a cushion.

MATERIALS

Piece of cherub fabric (This particular fabric is available in squares by mail order, worldwide, from my studio Artistic Renditions)

For the painting

Round or liner brush, size 0

Two ¼" flat brushes with stiff bristles, suitable for oil application

Note: One brush is used for the application of paint, the other to blend out the colour.

Winsor & Newton Artists Oil Colours: Flesh, Raw Sienna, Burnt Sienna Cadmium Red, Viridian Hue, Olive Green, Titanium White

Palette (a milk carton, flattened and cleaned, is fine)

Workboard

Clean white paper

Masking tape

For the embroidery

Embroidery threads in either variegated hand-dyed rayon yarn or Anchor Marlitt Thread: Green 895, Rust 864, Blue 1052, Grey 845, Gold 1013

A few small glass amber-coloured beads

Chenille needle

Beading needle

Water-soluble marker pen

Sharp HB pencil

PREPARATION

See the embroidery design on page 62.

STEP ONE

Using the pencil, lightly transfer the design to the fabric. A light box can make this easier. If you don't have a light box, tape the design to a window with the light coming through it. Tape the fabric over the top and trace the design. Place the fabric over the sheet of clean white paper and tape it down on the workboard.

STEP TWO

Prepare the palette, mixing the fabric medium with the paints following the manufacturer's instructions.

PAINTING

STEP ONE

Apply the skin tones, using Flesh with a touch of Burnt Sienna around the edges of the bodies, arms and legs. With the second brush, softly blend the colours across and around the contours of the bodies. Add extra Burnt Sienna where the shadows are deeper.

STEP TWO

Gently apply the paint to the edges of the face and softly contour it, bringing a touch more Flesh colour to the cheeks. Paint the eyes subtly with the liner brush and Burnt Sienna. Paint a dot for the highlight in Titanium White.

Stitch the garland thicker near the hands and tapering towards the ends.

61

STEP THREE

Paint the hair with Raw Sienna, adding depth with Burnt Sienna.

STEP FOUR

Paint the lips with the liner brush, using Cadmium Red.

STEP FIVE

Paint the wings and drapes with Viridian Hue, Titanium White and a touch of Raw Sienna, mixed together. The shadow colour is Olive Green.

STEP SIX

Allow the oil paints to dry thoroughly before adding the embroidery – this can take up to a week.

EMBROIDERY

STEP ONE

Mark a line across the heads of the cherubs and a circle for the wreath, using the sharp pencil or the water-soluble pen.

STEP TWO

Embroider the circlet, using the placement design and key, and referring to the stitch guide on pages 76–78.

Embroider the circlets and wreath in French knots and lazy daisy stitch, using 895, 864 and 845. The centres are worked in 1013. Embroider the leaves in lazy daisy stitch, using 1052 and 895.

STEP THREE

Using the beading needle, attach a few beads, scattering them through the circlet on the front cherub.

MAKING UP

Have your picture professionally framed for a perfect finish.

KEY

o   Bead

    French knot

    Lazy daisy

EMBROIDERY DESIGN

FLORALS

In this section, we look at painting flowers on fabric. I have incorporated some gorgeous flower designs in a variety of projects – some are embellished with embroidery, while others are shown as purely painted pieces.

No matter what the style of painting, I have included a line drawing guide for each project, which you will be able to adapt for your own use. Enlarge or reduce the size as desired.

If you are painting freehand, it may be necessary to mark in placement lines. For instance, if you are painting a circular design, mark in the circle. You may also need to mark in a design which has a limited area because of seams etc. Planning these designs can be quite important.

As I have mentioned previously, my first book, *Creative Inspirations in Paint*, covers all the technical information you will need for painting flowers, and you may find it helpful to refer to as a companion book.

PAINTING FLOWERS

• Remember to use three values of colour in your painting – light, medium and a depth tone. This is important to obtain an indication of the light source, as well as to give deeper colour in the shadowed areas. It will also help give dimension and shape to your work.
• Always introduce the background or leaf colour through the flowers. Use these colours for creating shadows and shaping.
• Make a conscious effort to load your brush with a shaded application of paint at all times.

• Make the flowers interesting by painting different shapes and angles, as well as painting them at different stages of growth.
• Experiment with creating your own designs. The best design of all is your own interpretation from life.

MCLOUGHLIN SPRING POSY

This lovely posy of daffodils, delphiniums and lily of the valley is painted on a self-patterned fabric. Strong white highlights against the bright flowers give this cushion a fresh feel, which is ideal for a sunroom or casual living area.

MATERIALS

40 cm (16 in) of pale green self-patterned fabric for the front
Note: The painted area is 38 cm (15 in) square.
1/4" brush
Liner brush, size 0
Jo Sonja's Textile Medium
Sharp HB pencil
Palette (a milk carton, flattened and cleaned, is fine)
Jar of water
Light box (optional)
Clean white paper
Workboard
Masking tape
Jo Sonja's Artists Acrylic Gouache: Cadmium Yellow, Cadmium Orange, Pine Green, Paynes Gray, Diox Purple, Ultramarine Blue, Titanium White
Mokuba Rayon Ribbon, 21 Blue
Sewing thread to match the ribbon and the fabric
40 cm (16 in) cushion insert

PREPARATION

See the painting design on the Pull Out Pattern Sheet.

STEP ONE

Using the pencil, lightly transfer the design to the fabric. A light box can make this easier. If you don't have a light box, tape the design to a window with the light coming through it. Tape the fabric over the top and trace the design. Place the fabric over the clean white paper and tape it down on the workboard.

STEP TWO

Prepare the palette, mixing the textile medium with the paints, following the manufacturer's instructions.

PAINTING

STEP ONE

Using the 1/4" brush, paint the daffodils with Cadmium Yellow and Cadmium Orange, shading with Pine Green and Paynes Gray.

STEP TWO

Paint the delphiniums with Diox Purple and Ultramarine Blue. Add highlights with Titanium White. Paint the leaves in Pine Green.

STEP THREE

Paint the lily of the valley with Titanium White, shadowed with Pine Green.

STEP FOUR

Remove the paper from the back of the fabric so that it doesn't stick when the paint dries. Allow the painting to dry completely, then heat-set it by ironing on the back of the fabric.

STEP FIVE

Tie a bow with the blue ribbon and sew it to the base of the posy, using the matching sewing thread.

MAKING UP

You can have your cushion professionally made up, as this one was, or you can make up the cushion yourself, following the general instructions for making cushions on page 8. If you do not wish to make a cushion, the design would look equally appealing as a framed picture.

Strong white highlights give a fresh feel.

BEADED WILDFLOWERS

This beautiful Australian wildflower painting by Jen McCallum has been beaded, padded and embroidered to enhance the stamens of the gumnuts and bottlebrush and give height and depth to the eye of the Sturt desert pea.

Not often painted on fabric, Australian wildflowers have a unique beauty which Jen McCallum certainly captures in her paintings. I was so taken with her work that I asked her to paint one of her original designs to be included in my book.

It makes a beautiful framed picture or it could be used to cover the lid of a box. It would also look lovely under glass as an inset for a table or firescreen. The design could be enlarged and a mount, either oval or rectangular, cut to suit.

MATERIALS

38 cm x 48 cm (15 in x 19 in) of
  calico
For the painting
$1/2$" flat brush
$1/4$" flat brush
Liner brush, size 0
Jo Sonja's Textile Medium
Jo Sonja's Artists Acrylic Gouache:
  Napthol Red Light, Burgundy,
  Yellow Light, Pine Green, Teal
  Green, Smoked Pearl, Burnt
  Umber, Raw Sienna, Paynes Gray,
  Carbon Black
Palette
Jar of water
Sharp HB pencil
Light box (optional)
Workboard
Masking tape
Clean white paper
For the embroidery
Chenille needles, various sizes
Beading needle
Small amber-coloured and clear
  beads
Anchor Marlitt Thread: Black, Gold
  869, Green 1011

PREPARATION

See the painting and embroidery design on page 69.

STEP ONE

Using the pencil, lightly transfer the design to the fabric. A light box can make this easier. See page 7 for the use of the light box and an alternative. Place the fabric over a sheet of the clean white paper and tape it down on the workboard.

STEP TWO

Prepare the pallette, mixing the fabric medium with the paints, following the manufacturer's instructions.

PAINTING

STEP ONE

Paint the Sturt's desert pea and the bottlebrush, using the $1/2$" brush and Napthol Red Light, Burgundy, Yellow Light and Raw Sienna. When painting the bottlebrush, use the chisel edge of the flat brush. The eye of the Sturt's

Amber beads give an added dimension to the stamens.

desert pea is painted in Carbon Black. The depth areas of the bottlebrush are painted in a mixture of Burnt Umber, Carbon Black and Paynes Gray.

STEP TWO

Paint the gumnut flowers in Napthol Red Light, Burgundy and Yellow Light and highlight the stamens in Raw Sienna and Smoked Pearl. The centres and the bell of the gumnuts are painted with the $1/4$" brush, using Pine Green and Raw Sienna with a touch of Burnt Umber for depth and Smoked Pearl for highlights.

STEP THREE

Paint the leaves in a smoky green which is a mix of Smoked Pearl and Pine Green with a touch of Paynes Gray, and Raw Sienna. Add depth with Pine Green, Burnt Umber and Paynes Gray and highlight with Smoked Pearl.

STEP FOUR

Using the liner brush, paint in the trailing stems, veins etc, using the photograph as a guide.

STEP FIVE

Remove the paper from the back of the fabric so that it doesn't stick when the paint dries. Allow the painting to dry completely, then heat-set it by ironing on the back of the fabric.

EMBROIDERY

STEP ONE

Using the beading needle, attach the small clear beads to areas on the small blossoms to indicate and reflect the stamens. Attach the amber beads on the large blossoms – they should look scattered and not too uniform.

The bottlebrush is painted with the chisel edge of the brush.

STEP TWO

With the Black Marlitt thread and a chenille needle, work satin stitch in the shape of the eye of the Sturt's desert pea.

STEP THREE

Using one strand each of 869 and 1011 together in a small chenille needle, work a few French knots at the ends of the bottlebrush flowers to indicate the stamens.

MAKING UP

Have your picture professionally framed and ask your framer to pad out the fabric slightly when mounting it.

KEY

Straight stitch

French knot

PAINTING AND EMBROIDERY DESIGN

MEDALLION OF ROSES

This design is painted on a cream moiré taffeta with a feature of three baby roses at the top and bottom of the medallion. The leafy trails extending from the roses intermingle to create the oval form. A nice addition to this design is to paint or embroider initials in the centre of the medallion.

MATERIALS

40 cm (16 in) of cream moiré taffeta
  for the front
Sharp HB pencil
1/4" square shader brush
Liner brush, size 00
Jar of water
Palette (a milk carton, cleaned and
  flattened, is fine)
Clean white paper
Workboard
Masking tape
Jo Sonja's Textile Medium
Jo Sonja's Artists Acrylic Gouache:
  Smoked Pearl, Burgundy, Raw
  Sienna, Paynes Gray, Pine Green,
  Teal Green
Braid (optional)

PREPARATION

See the painting design on the Pull Out Pattern Sheet.

STEP ONE

Using the pencil, lightly transfer the design to the fabric for the front. A light box can make this easier. If you don't have a light box, tape the design to a window with the light coming through it. Tape the fabric over the top and trace the design. Place the fabric over the clean white paper and tape it down on the workboard.

STEP TWO

Prepare the palette, mixing the textile medium with the paints, following the manufacturer's instructions.

PAINTING

STEP ONE

Using the 1/4" brush, paint the roses in Smoked Pearl as the light value colour, Burgundy mixed with Smoked Pearl and a touch of Raw Sienna for the mid-tone colour and Burgundy for the deep-value colour.

STEP TWO

Paint the buds, leaves and stems in Smoked Pearl and Pine Green.

STEP THREE

To define the medallion shape, I have brushed on shadowy leaves and used the liner brush to extend the stems as part of the design.

MAKING UP

Have your cushion professionally made up, as this one was, or you can make up the cushion yourself, using the general instructions for making cushions on page 8.

Paint the roses in three values of colour.

71

ROSE FOOTSTOOL

This footstool has a romantic look, upholstered with pink moiré taffeta which has been hand-painted with beautiful roses. An added touch of embroidery has given height to specific areas of the petals and leaves.

A light application of crosshatching with the ½" brush has given softness to the background.

The footstool has been trimmed with pompom fringing in a colour which coordinates with the fabric. The base has been stained with a cedar-coloured wood stain, but a variety of painted finishes would also be suitable. This design could also be used to make a beautiful cushion.

MATERIALS

Wooden footstool base, 28 cm (11 in) in diameter

For the painting

45 cm (18 in) square of moiré taffeta
90 cm (36 in) of braid or fringing
Sharp HB pencil
Jo Sonja's Artists Acrylic Gouache: Smoked Pearl, Raw Sienna, Burgundy, Pine Green, Teal Green, Paynes Gray
Jo Sonja's Textile Medium
½" flat brush
Liner brush, size 0
Palette (a milk carton, cleaned and flattened, is fine)
Jar of water
Light box (optional)
Workboard
Masking tape
Clean white paper

For the embroidery

Chenille needles
Scissors
Anchor Stranded Cotton: White, Cream; Pinks 892, 893; Blue/Green 231; Green 681

PREPARATION

See the painting and embroidery design on page 75.

STEP ONE

Using the pencil, lightly transfer the design to the fabric. A light box can make this easier. See page 7 for the use of the light box and an alternative. Place the fabric over the clean white paper and tape it down on the workboard, using masking tape.

STEP TWO

Prepare the palette, mixing the textile medium with the paints, following the manufacturer's instructions.

PAINTING

STEP ONE

Paint the design with the ½" brush, and use the liner brush for painting the stems. Paint the roses using Smoked Pearl for the light-value colour, Smoked Pearl with a touch of Burgundy and Raw Sienna for the

Satin stitch at random over the petal turn backs.

mid-value colour and a mixture of Burgundy and Raw Sienna for the dark-value colour. Shadow areas across the roses with a mixture of Pine Green and Paynes Gray.

STEP TWO

Paint the leaves and background with a smoky green, which is achieved by mixing Pine Green and Smoked Pearl with a touch of Raw Sienna and Paynes Gray.

STEP THREE

Remove the paper from the back of the fabric so that it doesn't stick when the paint dries. Allow the painting to dry completely, then heat-set it by ironing on the back of the fabric.

EMBROIDERY

STEP ONE

Use the design as a guide for the embroidery. Embroider the roses, referring to the key and the stitch glossary on pages 76–78. Using all six strands of White and 892, embroider satin stitches in the shape of the turn backs on the rose petals.

STEP TWO

Work bullion stitches, French knots and rosettes in 893 and 892.

STEP THREE

Embroider the calyx and straight stitch leaves in 231. Work straight stitches in 681 to raise areas on the leaves to indicate height and veins.

MAKING UP

I thoroughly recommend having your piece professionally upholstered.

Clusters of rosettes, bullion stitches and French knots add interest.

Thread rosette

Bullion stitch bud

Satin stitch

Lazy daisy stitch

Fly stitch

PAINTING AND EMBROIDERY DESIGN
AND KEY

75

STITCH GLOSSARY

BLANKET STITCH

Bring the thread up through the fabric at **A**. Take it back down at **B** and up again at **C**, keeping the thread under the needle tip (Fig. 1).

To work this stitch in a circle for use in such flowers as hollyhocks, mark the circle with a pencil then, starting on the marked edge, work blanket stitches into the centre point. Continue working until you have completed stitching the circle (Fig. 2).

For the leaf shape, such as for the sunflower leaves, mark out the shape of the leaf in pencil then, starting at the top of the leaf and coming back to that point each time, work around the shape as before (Fig. 3).

LAZY DAISY STITCH

This stitch is often used for flowers and leaves. Bring the needle up at **A**, loop it around to **B**, entering the fabric as near as possible to **A**, keeping the thread under the needle. Make a small, straight stitch over the loop to anchor it (Fig. 4).

BULLION STITCH

This stitch is most commonly used for buds and roses. Bring the needle up at **A**, take it back down at **B** and up at **A** again, but do not pull the thread taut. This becomes the length of the stitch.

While the needle is protruding at **A**, wrap the thread loosely around it (Fig. 5). The number of wraps will determine the size of the bullion. Gently pull the needle through the looped threads, easing the wraps down onto the fabric. Take the needle back down to anchor the stitch at **B** (Fig. 6).

To make a bud, repeat this stitch three times bringing the ends close together (Fig. 7). They can be joined with a fly stitch for a calyx.

For a full rose, work the centre section with two or three straight bullion stitches. For the outside petals, lay the stitches in a circle around the centre, staggering their placement (Fig. 8). Most commonly, there are two rounds of bullion stitches around the centre, shading from dark to light.

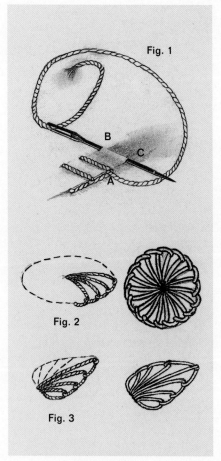

Fig. 1

Fig. 2

Fig. 3

Blanket stitch

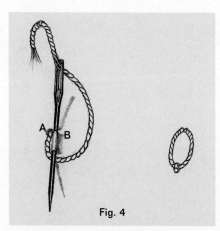

Lazy daisy stitch

Fig. 4

Fig. 5

Fig. 6

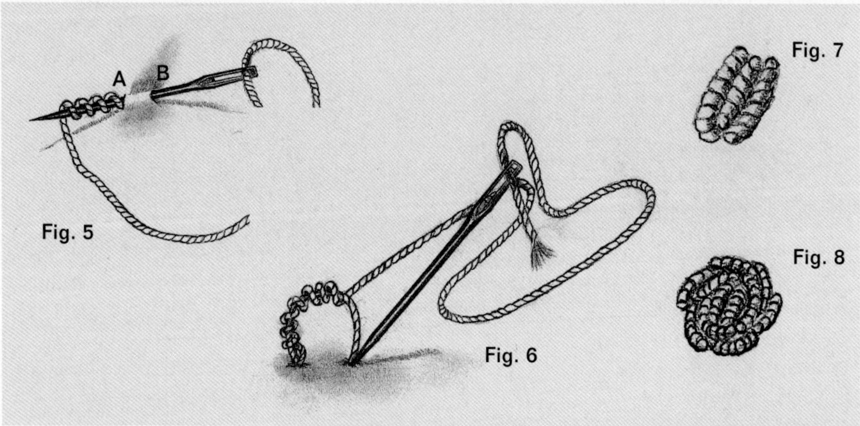

Bullion stitch

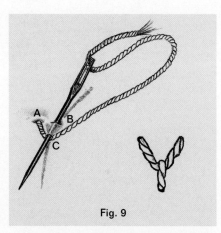

Fig. 9

Fly stitch

Fig. 7

Fig. 8

FLY STITCH

This stitch is used for working calyxes and leafy effects.

Bring the needle up through the fabric at **A**, down at **B** and out again at **C**, keeping the thread under the tip of the needle (Fig. 9). Pull the thread over the V shape and anchor it with a small straight stitch.

FRENCH KNOT

French knots are used for flowers, centres, trailing effects and buds, etc. Bring the needle through the fabric and wind the thread twice around the needle (Fig. 10). Take the needle back through the fabric as close as possible to the entry point, easing the knot down onto the fabric (Fig. 11). Pull the thread through to the back of the fabric and secure it, leaving the knot sitting on the fabric (Fig. 12).

RIBBON STITCH

Ribbon stitch can be used for the petals of flowers or for leaves (Figs 14 and 15). When working with ribbon, it is useful to secure the ribbon to the needle. Do this by threading the needle with the ribbon, then pulling it through the end of the ribbon to secure it.

To work a ribbon stitch, bring the ribbon through the fabric, then take the needle back through the ribbon where you wish the stitch to end (Fig. 13). Keep the stitch soft, making a pucker for petals or keeping it flat for leaves. Pull the ribbon through both thicknesses until it forms a nicely shaped peak with the turn-back.

RIBBON ROSE

The ribbon rose is hand-made, then attached to the fabric. It is usually used as a feature. Begin by turning down the raw end of the ribbon and winding it five times to form the base (Fig. 16). Secure with a few stitches at the bottom (Fig. 17). Place the flowing end of the ribbon over your thumb and twist the ribbon back and over, turning the base forward onto twisted ribbon to make a petal. Secure it at the base (Fig. 18). Each twist and fold becomes a petal. Continue until the desired size is reached (Fig. 19). Cut the end of the ribbon and stitch it under the rose. Hand-sew the ribbon rose in place.

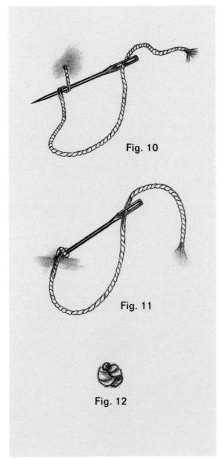

French knot

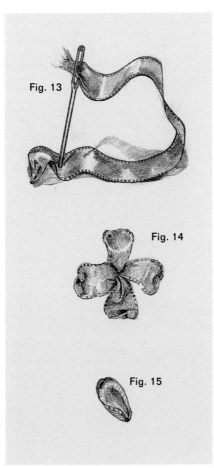

Ribbon stitch

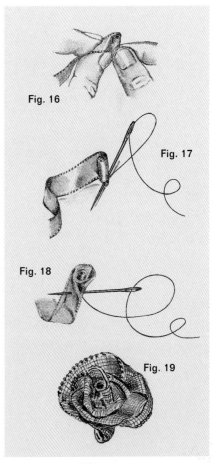

Ribbon rose

ROSETTE

Rosettes can be made from silk ribbon (Fig. 22) or thread (Fig. 21). They are used quite frequently in this book. The stitch is worked like a stem stitch, but is taken around in a circle, continually spiralling toward the centre (Fig. 20). Begin by marking a circle the size of the rose. When you reach the centre point, leave a slightly raised loop before taking the thread or ribbon through to the back to anchor it.

SATIN STITCH

Satin stitch is a series of parallel stitches worked closely together to block in a shape (Fig. 23) – for example, the turn backs of the roses on the footstool on page 72 (Fig. 24).

STRAIGHT STITCH

For a straight stitch, simply bring the needle up at **A** and down at **B** (Fig. 26). Different length stitches and placements create new effects. For example, straight stitch daisy (Fig. 27) is created by using the straight stitch method within a circle. Begin by marking the circle at the desired size, then work straight stitches from the centre point to the marked outer line (Fig. 25). It is helpful to divide the circle into four segments and work each quarter at a time. Add a French knot to the centre.

STEM STITCH

Stem stitch is most often used to create a stitched line (Fig. 29). Bring the needle through the fabric, pointing it away from the direction you are working. Make a stitch, then take the needle halfway back along the first stitch (Fig. 28). Continue to follow the stitch line, making the next stitch half the size of the first one and bringing the needle back to the end of the first stitch. Remember to keep the thread under the needle as you go.

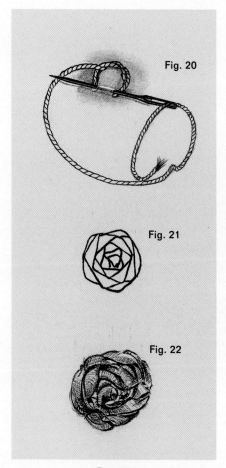

Rosette

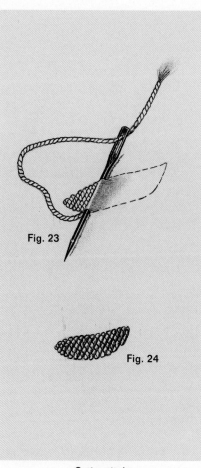

Satin stitch

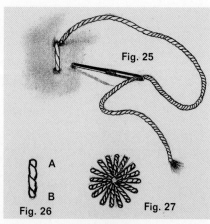

Straight stitch

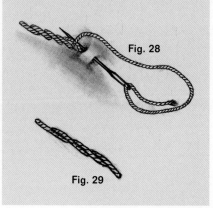

Stem stitch

This gorgeous quilt combines hand-painted blocks and borders with traditional quilting.

ACKNOWLEDGMENTS

Foremost, to my family for their ongoing support and effort; their own creativeness, understanding and patience, and especially to Malcolm, for again contributing his wonderful illustrations for the stitch glossary – I thank you with all my heart.

To my very dear friend Robyn Christou, who has given me so much help, support and assistance at the studio over the last couple of years, I thank you so much.

To my very special friends and colleagues, Kirry Toose, Kaye Pyke and Sue Dickens – thank you for your friendship and support.

To the studios throughout Australia where I conduct workshops and to my many students who attend each year, I would like to thank all of you for your ongoing support and friendship: Kirry Toose of Kirry Toose Design, Cowan, NSW; Kay Pyke of Kaye Pyke, Port Melbourne, Victoria; Sue Schirmer of the Victorian Academy of Decorative Arts, Camberwell, Victoria; Yvonne Brown of Handcrafts R Us, Canberra, ACT; Vicky Nicholson of WA Folk Art, Western Australia; Shaen Faulkner of Junee, NSW; the Brisbane girls; Francis Mason, Katunga, Victoria.

A special thank you to the very special people who contributed to the projects in this book: Jen McCallum, an artist in her own right who was a dedicated student of my style of decorative art and later became my main painting teacher at Artistic Renditions Studio – thank you so much for your contribution to the studio and your loyalty as a teacher and friend. Thank you for your wonderful quilt on page 79 and beautiful wildflower painting, which I am pleased to include in this book.

Mary Jaquier who came to me as a very talented embroiderer wanting to learn painted backgrounds – thank you so much for your beautiful work, represented by the 'Autumn Leaves' and 'Poppies' projects.

Sue Turrell, thank you for your beautiful embroidery in our cottage project, 'Jessie's House', as well as for helping me on many other occasions with embroidery projects when time was running out.

Kirry Toose, thank you for contributing the instructions for your own special style of cushion making. Thanks also to:

Denise McLoughlin and Doris Connelly, for your continued support; Marlene Hoare for your support and assistance, and Sue Schirmer for cutting the stencil to my pansy design.

McLOUGHLIN SPRING POSY
Painting Design

AUTUMN LEAVES
Painting and Stencil Design

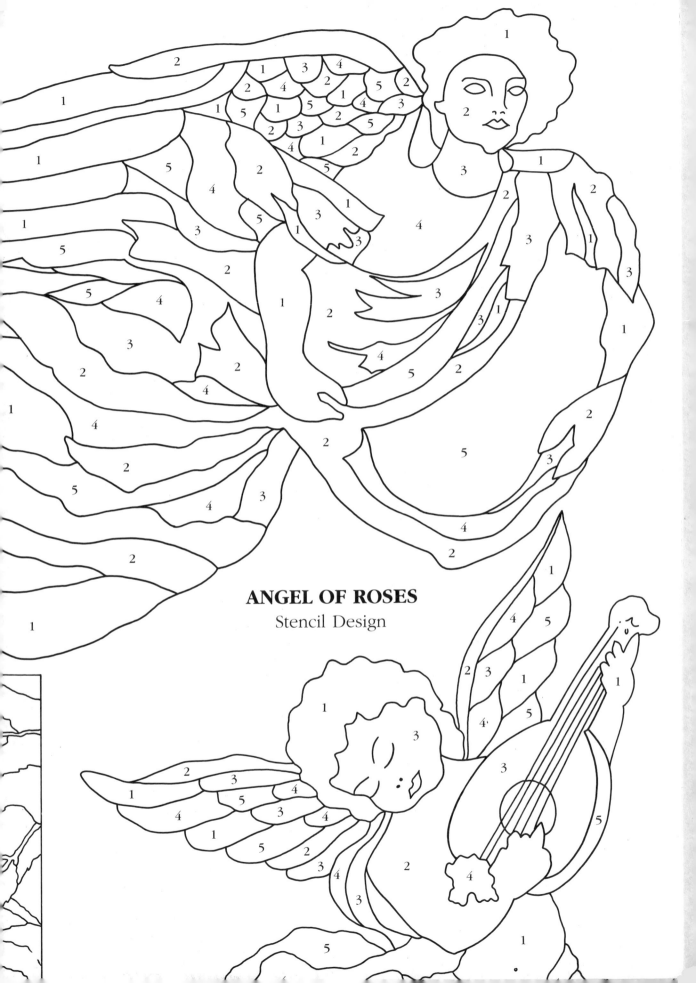

ANGEL OF ROSES
Stencil Design